MW00885961

PARfessionals'
Peer Recovery/Addictions Recovery Coach Training

HOME STUDY COURSE

Home Study Course

Course Description

This course is designed to be comprehensive and prepare students for Recovery Support certification. It will cover background knowledge including history of the recovery movement, the knowledge needed to become a peer supporter or a recovery coach, models of recovery, ethics how to create recovery partnerships, assess clients, create recovery and relapse prevention plans. The course will end with a practical discussion on finding a job as a recovery support professional.

Intended Audience

Those interested in becoming recovery support professionals within a behavioral health or treatment system.

Course Goals and Objectives

- ✓ To gain knowledge about the roles, core competencies, and ethics of peer supporters and addiction recovery coaches.
- ✓ To identify addiction recovery models, become knowledgeable about the similarities and differences between each, and how they can be used in a peer support context.
- ✓ To identify and use basic techniques peer support specialists utilize such as assessments, motivational interviewing, documentation, recovery planning, and relapse prevention plans.
- ✓ To guide a client through first meetings, assessments, goal setting, and recovery planning.
- ✓ To utilize self-awareness skills to interact with clients in a professional, ethical manner, serving as an example of recovery success.
- ✓ To demonstrate cultural competency, self-advocacy as well as personal and professional growth.

Course Expectations

All students must read the material, complete the activities, pass the final exam, and complete a course exit survey.

Materials Needed

- ✓ PARfessionals Study Guide
- ✓ Philadelphia Behavioral Health Services Transformation: Practice Guidelines for Recovery and Resilience Oriented Treatment, Department of Behavioral Health and Intellectual Disability Services available for free download on www.dbhids.org.

Course Evaluation

- ✓ Personal reflection project (Appendix C)
- ✓ Sample client project (Appendix D)
- ✓ Advocacy project optional (Appendix E)

KNOWLEDGE
Course Overview

Lesson Topics

Course Goals & Expectations
Recovery Talk
    What is recovery?
    Importance of lived experience
    Personal attributes of peer support
    Recovery environment qualities

Recovery is a process clouded with connotations. For some, recovery is lined with hope, while others have experienced seemingly never ending storms. Understanding the many definitions, the many connotations, the many subjective experiences involved in this one little word sets the foundation for an attitude of openness when joining another in a recovery journey. Sharing experience in recovery can make a lasting impression, especially in the context of providing peer support. Increasing one's level of self-awareness and understanding what makes recovery more likely to succeed will increase the effectiveness of the peer support provided.

    ✓ To understand the importance of lived experience as a recovery resource.
    ✓ To identify personal attributes that make a good peer support professional.
    ✓ To identify qualities of a supportive, effective recovery community.

Reading

+ *Study Guide: Recovery Talk*
+ *Philadelphia - Appendix B: Toward a Clear Understanding of Recovery and Resilience*
+ *Lived Experience*
+ *VIA Classification of Character Strengths (Appendix A)*
+ *Characteristics of Good Peer Support,* Oakden & McKregg 2009
    ☆ *Executive Summary and Appendix A (the rest of the publication is optional)*
+ *Equipping Behavioral Health Systems & Authorities to Promote Peer Specialist/Peer Recovery Coaching Services,* BRSS TACS, 2012
    ☆ p. 5-8 Challenges section and p. 16-17 Future directions section (the rest of the publication is optional)

Recovery Talk
What is recovery? List some thoughts based upon your own experience.

_____

_____

_____

_____

_____

Importance of lived experience

Refer to Lived Experience handout and reflect on your own. Why is lived experience or experiential knowledge important for a peer supporter to have?

_____

_____

_____

Personal attributes of peer support

Create a list of *personal a*ttributes that would make a successful peer support professional.

1. _____

2. _____

3. _____

4. _____

5. _____

ACTIVITY: List 3 strengths from the VIA Classification of Strengths (Appendix A) that you obtained because of your lived experience. How will those strengths benefit you as a peer supporter?

_____

_____

_____

_____

_____

_____

_____

_____

_____

Recovery environment qualities

Create a list of **environment qualities** that would contribute to a successful peer support program.

1. _____

2. _____

3. _____

4. _____

5. _____

QUIZ

1. Recovery means restoring to health and is accomplished:
   a) in 30-60 days.
   b) in very few people.
   c) through a process of lifestyle changes.
   d) by making someone do what they are supposed to do.

2. The following are attributes of a good peer support professional except:
   a) open-mindedness.
   b) self-awareness.
   c) example of successful recovery.
   d) willing to push someone beyond their limits.

Joe is a peer support professional and he works at a local treatment center where his job is to greet people when they come in for information and engage them in the intake process. A client comes into the treatment center and the small waiting area is crowded. There are several people waiting who brought their kids. The kids are unruly and making a bunch of noise with no correction. There is a television on with the volume turned up to be heard over the noise of the kids and there is no seating left. The client timidly walks up to Joe's desk and her anxiety is visible all over her face. Joe is on the phone and turns away, ignoring the client. She stands there waiting for Joe to notice she is there and it becomes obvious to her that he is on a personal call. Impatient and nervous, she waves her hand to get Joe's attention and says, "I really need some help." Joe waves her away, gives her a dirty look and says "I'm on the phone! Go wait over there and someone will be with you in a bit."

Based on your lived experience, had you been the client, what would your reaction have been to this situation?

_____

_____

_____

Where did Joe go wrong?

_____

_____

_____

What environmental attribute could the treatment center have addressed to engage this client?

_____

_____

_____

Addiction Science Basics

Addiction science basics

Why can some people quit using their substance of choice cold turkey and some can't? That question has plagued addiction science researchers and research is finally yielding some answers. Learn how addiction effects the brain and how those effects influence recovery.

- ✓ Understand how addiction changes the brain.
- ✓ Understand how the physical nature of addiction affects recovery.

Reading/Assignment

- ✦ *Study Guide: Addiction Science basics*
- ✦ NIDA Publication—*Drugs, Brains, and Behavior: The Science of Addiction*

How does addiction change the brain?

_____

_____

_____

_____

_____

_____

_____

_____

_____

_____

_____

_____

_____

_____

_____

_____

QUIZ

1. Most drugs of abuse target the brain's reward system by flooding the circuits with _____

    a) dopamine.
    b) seratonin.
    c) epinephrine.
    d) drugs.

2. Chronic exposure to drugs of abuse disrupts the brain's ability to control and inhibit behaviors leading to

    a) psychosis.
    b) tolerance and dependence.
    c) brain damage.
    d) none of the above.

What are 2 ways a peer supporter can use addiction science to help a client understand recovery better?

_____

_____

_____

_____

_____

Name two ways a peer supporter can help a client develop their natural ability to feel pleasure.

_____

_____

_____

_____

_____

History of the Recovery Movement

Lesson Topics

History of Recovery Movement
(optional) Canadian History of Recovery and addiction treatment
　　　　Addiction Recovery Models
　　　　Minnesota Model
　　　　The Harm Reduction Model (ATA)
　　　　12-step and mutual aid groups

The recovery community has a rich history, mostly led by those in recovery. That history has contributed to several models of recovery that have served as the foundation for current models.

✓ Identify key figures of the recovery movement and their contribution to the field.
✓ Explain the development of the recovery movement.
✓ Understand the different addiction recovery models, how they are similar and how they differ.

Reading

✦ *Study Guide: History of Recovery Movement*
✦ *A Chronology of Moderation Societies and Related Controversies.* William White
✦ *History of Addiction Treatment Services,* William White

Minnesota Model: List key concepts.

_____

_____

_____

_____

The Harm Reduction Model (ATA): List key concepts.

_____

_____

_____

_____

12-step and mutual aid groups: List key concepts.

_____

_____

_____

_____

QUIZ

1. What happened in the 1940's and 1950's that hindered the recovery movement?

   a) People were poor and couldn't afford treatment.
   b) Institutionalization as the primary form of treatment.
   c) World War II.
   d) None of the above.

2. Which recovery models believe that substance abuse is an involuntary chronic disease?

   a) Minnesota Model.
   b) Recovery Management Model.
   c) Harm Reduction Model.
   d) a and b.

3. Which recovery model focuses on the harm done by the drug, not abstinence?

   a) Minnesota Model.
   b) Recovery Management Model.
   c) Harm Reduction Model.
   d) 12 Step Mutual Aid.

4. Alcoholics Anonymous (AA) is the standard by which all other mutual aid societies are judged.

   a) True.
   b) False.

5. Which recovery model served as a forerunner for peer support being integrated into treatment?

   a) Minnesota Model.
   b) Recovery Management Model.
   c) Harm Reduction Model.
   d) 12 Step Mutual Aid.

History of Addiction Treatment

Lesson Topics

History of addiction treatment
What we know about addiction science and treatment outcomes
Introduction of SAMHSA Definition of Recovery and ROSC
Systems of Recovery
Integrated care (behavioral health and medical)

In order for peer recovery specialists to understand their value to the recovery community and current treatment models, it's important to know where substance abuse treatment has been, where it's going, how it's been effective, what's not been effective, and what is being done to make it more effective.

- ✓ To understand the evolution of addiction treatment.
- ✓ To know how research supports recovery oriented systems of care and peer support

Reading

+ *Study Guide: History of Addiction Treatment*
+ *SAMHSA Working Definition of Recovery*
+ *Philadelphia: Section 1 Introduction, Section 2 Overview of the Framework*
+ *Recovery Management and Recovery Oriented Systems of Care,* William White
  - Chapters 1, 2 and 5 (the rest is optional). *This publication offers a comprehensive look at substance abuse treatment and states the case for ROSC*

List benefits and drawbacks of each model.

Acute Care Model	Chronic Care Model

Why aren't more people getting treatment?

_____

_____

_____

_____

_____

SAMHSA's Definition of Recovery

A _____ of _____ through which individuals improve their
_____ and _____, live a _____ life, and strive to reach their
_____.

Four Dimensions of Recovery

1. _____
2. _____
3. _____
4. _____

Ten Guiding Principles of Recovery

1. _____
2. _____
3. _____
4. _____
5. _____
6. _____
7. _____
8. _____
9. _____
10. _____

Recovery-oriented systems of care refers to the complete network of indigenous and professional services and relationships that can support the long-term recovery of individuals and families and the creation of values and policies in the larger cultural and policy environment that are supportive of these recovery processes.

Recovery management is a philosophy of organizing addiction treatment and recovery support services to enhance pre-recovery engagement, recovery initiation, long-term recovery maintenance, and the quality of personal/family life in long-term recovery.

QUIZ

1. Why did treatment providers in the 1970's and 1980's mold services to look like the
    medical model?

    a)   To provide more jobs.
    b)   To legitimize treatment and secure funding.
    c)   To make things difficult for clients.

    List 2 benefits and 2 challenges of the acute care model.

    _____

    _____

    _____

    _____

    _____

2. The current addiction recovery model is based upon what kind of care model?

    a)   Circular.
    b)   Chronic disease.
    c)   Never ending.

    List 2 reasons more people aren't getting treatment.

    _____

    _____

    _____

    _____

    _____

3. A complete network of indigenous and professional services and relationships that can
    support the long-term recovery of individuals and families and the creation of values and
    policies in the larger cultural and policy environment that are supportive of these recovery
    processes is called:

    a)   Recovery management.
    b)   Recovery-oriented systems of care.
    c)   Chronic disease model.

Peer Support Defined

Lesson Topics

What is Peer Support and how does it fit into current treatment models?
Types of Peer Support
Core competencies
Of peer support
Of recovery coaches
Integrated behavioral health and primary care

The legitimacy and importance of peer support has developed out of research and a desire to provide effective, comprehensive addiction treatment services. Just as there are many definitions of recovery, so there are the definitions of "peer support" and what peer support entails. In an effort to create standardization, several organizations have taken the lead in outlining the core competencies of peer support professionals.

✓ Become familiar with the history of the recovery movement and how peer recovery services fit into current systems.
✓ Define the role of a peer recovery coach.
✓ Identify the types of recovery coaches; give examples of the duties of each.
✓ Understand the core competencies and basic knowledge required for recovery coaches and peer support recovery specialists.

Reading

✦ *Study Guide: Peer Support Defined*
✦ *Review Core Competencies from IC&RC, ICF, RCI, iNAPS, SAMHSA-HRSA Center for Integrated Health Solutions (CIHS)*
✦ *What are peer recovery support services?* US HHS Pub 2009

What is peer support and how does it fit into current treatment models?

_____

_____

_____

_____

_____

Core competencies self-assessment

Evaluate your current level of competency as a peer supporter. What areas do you need to work on? How do you plan to get there?

_____

_____

_____

_____

_____

QUIZ

1. None of the types of peer support roles require a license or certification.

    a) True.
    b) False.

2. The term peer recovery support specialist is often used interchangeably in the field with the terms recovery coach, peer mentor, recovery support practitioner, care manager or recovery specialist.

    a) True.
    b) False.

3. A good peer support specialist is often in recovery themselves, so they know what steps made recovery successful.

    a) True.
    b) False.

Which core competencies (up to 2) did you find most important for a peer support specialist to possess and why?

_____

_____

_____

_____

_____

_____

_____

_____

_____

_____

Ethics

In order to provide the highest quality services and maintain the legitimacy of the profession, peer supporters are expected to abide by standards of conduct. When peer supporters adhere to high standards of conduct, clients can have confidence in the consistency and quality of services they receive.

✓ Understand professional ethics and how they relate to the peer support specialist and recovery coach relationship.
✓ Define confidentiality and how it relates to the recovery and treatment community.
✓ Demonstrate the key components of documentation.
✓ Importance of continued ethics education.

Reading

+ *Study Guide: Ethics*
+ *Ethical Guidelines for the Delivery of Peer-based Recovery Support Services (Great Lakes. ATTC publication)*
+ *ICF Code of Ethics*
+ *RCI Code of Ethics*
+ *iNAPS Code of Ethics*
+ *Legal Overview for Peer Supporters by* Greg Samurovich, Esq
+ *HIPAA for Dummies*
+ *Substance Abuse & Confidentiality 42 CFR Part 2*
+ *Everything you ever wanted to know about casenotes*

Boundaries
Define boundaries:

_____

ACTIVITY: Take the Boundary Assessment (Appendix B). Write down 3 ways you plan to protect your boundaries.

1. _____
2. _____
3. _____

QUIZ

Jim has been a peer support specialist in the field for nearly 2 years. He is well respected by his community and co-workers. Recently Jim has been arriving late to work and canceling appointments on short notice. He has been irritable and impatient with his co-workers and they suspect he has begun a romantic relationship with a client.

1. Which ethical principle is Jim violating?
    a) Boundaries.
    b) Professional limitation.
    c) confidentiality.

Read the following case example and provide a D.A.P note based on the information given.

Crystal is a 24 year old female that was charged with a DUI. This event brought her to seek treatment at an inpatient treatment facility. After her discharge she began seeking the help of a peer support specialist on a weekly basis. At her second session she states that she feels she is already making progress towards her goals. She states she is "motivated and that is all that it takes". Since her first session she did complete the homework given to her by coming up with at least 5 job leads and completed the Wheel of Life which demonstrated that her life is off balance financially. Without a job Crystal expected these results and has a goal to strengthen this area. Next week she hopes that these job leads will turn into interviews.

D _____

   _____

A _____

   _____

P _____

   _____

Emmy, a peer support specialist, was walking down the hall when a client stopped her and said "Dr. Emmy, I would like to set up a time to talk about my depression." Emmy states that she is available later in the day and schedules an appointment with the client.

2. Which ethical principle is Jim violating?
    a) Boundaries.
    b) Professional limitation.
    c) confidentiality.

How can Emmy fix the ethical problem?

_____

_____

_____

Alvin is a busy peer support specialist. After completing a meeting with a client for program participation, which included a consent form in which confidentiality was fully addressed, he left the file open on his desk. He hoped to work on the files over his lunch break when he had some extra time to update the notes. He locked his door so that the files were secure. Alvin ran a bit late meeting his next scheduled client and immediately brought them back to his office. As they sat down, the client looked at Alvin's desk and said "I know that guy. We used to work together many years ago," and pointed at the file which had a name listed clearly on the side. He then asks Alvin, "How is he doing?" Alvin says that because of confidentiality he is unable to disclose information about the family.

1.   What ethical principle has been violated?

   a)   Boundaries.
   b)   Professional limitation.
   c)   confidentiality.

What could Alvin do to prevent this from happening again?

_____

_____

_____

_____

CREATING PARTNERSHIP
Phases of Peer Support & Basic Skills

Lesson Topics

Phases of Peer Support
Basic Skills:
Communication and effective listening
Stages of Change introduction
Motivational Interviewing (MI)
Cognitive Distortions

Relationships go through phases and client-centered services are enhanced by basic therapeutic relationship skills. Learn how to communicate and listen to clients effectively and begin to understand how to motivate others to change.

✓ Identify the phases of the peer support process.
✓ Understand basic skills needed to facilitate relationships such as questioning and active listening.
✓ Understand and apply stages of change.
✓ Understand and learn the basic skills of motivational interviewing.
✓ Learn to identify and reframe cognitive distortions.

Reading

Required:
+ *Study Guide: Phases of Peer Support & Basic Skillsl Skills, Cognitive Distortions*
+ *Active Listening Chart*
+ *MI Basics*
+ *Stages of Change MI*
+ *MI Skills Tip Sheet*

Phases of peer support

1. _____
2. _____
3. _____
4. _____
5. _____
6. _____

Six Stages of Change

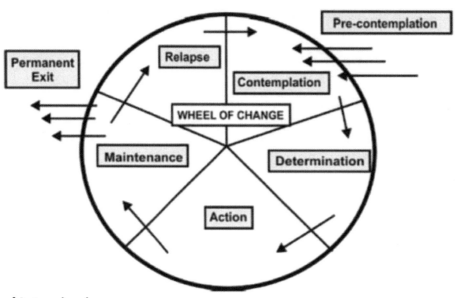

Motivational Interviewing

Spirit of MI is based upon 3 elements

1. _____
2. _____
3. _____

Four principles of MI

1. _____
2. _____
3. _____
4. _____

MI Skills

O_ _____
A_ _____
R_ _____
S_ _____

QUIZ

1. An active listening skill where a peer supporter would restate perceptions of what the client said based upon cues heard or perceived by listening to what is not said is called:

   a) Listening.
   b) Summarizing.
   c) Reflecting.
   d) Self-management.

2. In this stage of change, a client may acknowledge there is a problem, but is not quite prepared to make change happen:

   a) Precontemplation.
   b) Contemplation.
   c) Preparation.
   d) Action.
   e) Maintenance.
   f) Relapse.

3. In this stage of change, a peer supporter would start helping the client develop goals.

   a) Precontemplation.
   b) Contemplation.
   c) Preparation.
   e) Maintenance.
   f) Relapse.

4. The goal for motivational interviewing is for the client to reach their own conclusion about their substance use.

   a) True.
   b) False.

5. Which of the following principle are NOT a part of motivational interviewing?

   a) Expressing empathy.
   b) Supporting self-efficacy.
   c) Rolling with resistance.
   d) Making comparisons.
   e) Developing discrepancy.

Group Facilitation

Basic group facilitation

Peer supporters are an integral part of demonstrating successful recovery skills and are often invited to participate in group facilitation. Groups are an effective means for people in recovery to practice skills they are learning and build recovery-oriented social support.

    ✓   Learn basic group facilitation skills.

Reading/Assignment

    ✦   *Study Guide: Group Facilitation Basics*

Group Types

    ✓ _____

    ✓ _____

    ✓ _____

    ✓ _____

Skills necessary for group facilitation

    ✓ _____

    ✓ _____

    ✓ _____

    ✓ _____

    ✓ _____

    ✓ _____

If you are or will be expected to facilitate a support or an education group, ***it is highly recommended that you get training for doing so.*** Group facilitation is an art whether you are a lead or a co-facilitator. Group members will respond and thrive in well run groups and group that are well run are dependent upon the skills of the facilitator.

QUIZ

1. In which type of group does the facilitator focus on making sure group members have opportunities to participate and promotes group interaction?

    a) Psychoeducational group
    b) Support group
    c) Therapy group

Which skill do you feel is most important for a peer support specialist to facilitate groups?

_____

_____

_____

First Meeting & Assessment

Lesson Topics	First Meeting and assessment
	Assessment Basics and Purpose
	Ethics of Assessment
	Suggested Assessments

Not only do first impressions set the stage for a therapeutic relationships, but the first meeting also serves as an opportunity for a peer supporter to learn about a clients' needs.

- ✓ Examine the initial stage of contact as it relates to the recovery community.
- ✓ Understand basic ethical use of assessments and their purpose.
- ✓ Acquire knowledge about assessment methods and instruments used in the substance abuse recovery field.
- ✓ Create protocol for assessing clients .
- ✓ Identify ways in which a client's personal narrative can help a client resolve their issues.

Reading

- ✦ *Study Guide: Assessment*
- ✦ *Philadelphia: Section 3 Domain 1 and 2; Appendix F: Person-first Assessment*

What makes a good first meeting?

_____

_____

_____

_____

Types of assessment

- ✓ _____
- ✓ _____
- ✓ _____
- ✓ _____

QUIZ

1. The overall goal of the first session is to identify the client's stage of change.

    a) True.
    b) False.

2. During the initial contact the peer support specialist should utilize passive listening and motivational interviewing techniques.

    a) True.
    b) False.

3. Assessments should only occur during the initial stages of recovery and are not necessary to be performed in an ongoing manner.

    a) True.
    b) False.

4. An example of an assessment that can be used to determine the client's current coping skills:

    a) MBTI.
    b) General Self-Efficacy Scale.
    c) Brief COPE.
    d) Mini-Screen.

5. Peer supporters often give IQ tests and personality assessments such as the MMPI.

    a) True.
    b) False.

Why or why not?

_____

_____

_____

_____

Co-occurring Disorders & MAT

Co-occurring Disorders
Medication Assisted Treatment (MAT)
Suicide/Self harm assessment

In an effort to provide more effective comprehensive treatment services, more attention is being paid to co-occurring disorders and medication assisted treatment. Peer supporters should have the basic skills to help identify clients who need more comprehensive services and refer them to qualified help.

- ✓ Identify when and how to refer a client for counseling for co-occurring disorders.
- ✓ Understand the benefits, barriers, and basics of medication assisted treatment.
- ✓ Learn basic suicide and self-harm screening

Reading/Assignment

- ✦ *Study guide: Co-occurring disorders, Medication Assisted Treatment (MAT)*
- ✦ *Transcript of Med Assisted Treatment SAMHSA video*
- ✦ *Suicide Risk Assess SAMHSA*

Define co-occurring disorders and give an example:

_____

_____

_____

_____

_____

Medication-Assisted Therapies.

Benefits	Barriers/Challenges

List 3 warning signs of suicide or self-harm and state what you would do if a client presented to you with these signs:

_____

_____

_____

_____

_____

QUIZ

1. A client should first seek treatment for their mental illness and then their substance abuse disorder.
    a)   True.
    b)   False.

2. Problems and consequences associated with co-occurring disorders include:
    a)   Relationship problems.
    b)   Financial problems.
    c)   High risk behavior.
    d)   Recurring relapse.
    e)   All of the above

3. A client comes to you after being released from a 5 day hospital stay for opiate detoxification. During your initial meeting, the client states she got started with opiates because she couldn't turn her brain off and describes it as "brain buzzing." After further exploration, you discover she may have been experiencing auditory hallucinations. Which of the following might you do?

    a)   Tell your client the brain buzzing will go away in time.
    b)   Have your client do a Modified Mini Screen to get more information and invite your client to meet with a therapist you know who might be able to help her.
    c)   Ignore what the client said and start into recovery planning.
    d)   None of the above.

4. Medication can solve an addiction problem all by itself.
    a)   True.
    b)   False.

When assessing for suicide, what signs should you look for?

_____

_____

_____

Whole Health Recovery

Whole Health Recovery

Substance use does not occur in a vacuum, nor does the recovery process. Humans are complex creatures and human behavior is even more complex. What works for one person in recovery may not work for another, and for some, only focusing on the substance use problem will only set them up for relapse. While discovery of the underlying issues may take time or another professional, as a peer recovery specialist, you can help clients understand that recovery is a lifestyle change. Guiding them through planning for whole-person recovery from a wellness perspective can help them with the lifestyle changes needed for recovery success.

✓ To understand and describe what whole health recovery means.
✓ To understand what role peer support can play in integrated healthcare.

Reading/Assignment

+ *Study guide: Whole Health Recovery*
+ *WHAM_CIHS Participant Guide*
+ *Personal medicine worksheet whole health version*

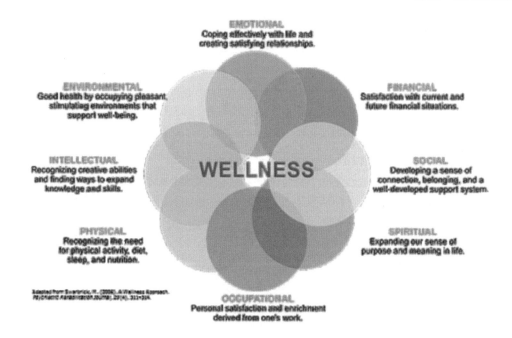

Read the WHAM CIHS Participant Guide and describe how you would use this approach with a client:

_____

_____

_____

Self-care

Compassion fatigue, self-care and self-assessment
Integrating your recovery story into peer support
Serving as a recovery example

INot only do peer supporters need to continue to take care of themselves and their own recovery, but they are an example of a recovery lifestyle to their clients.
- ✓ To understand the importance of self-care and create self-care plans in advance.
- ✓ To understand how one's recovery is integrated into peer support and using one's recovery as an example to clients.

Reading/Assignment

+ *Study Guide: Self-Care*
+ *Recognizing Compassion Fatigue handout*
+ *Self-care Defined handout*

ACTIVITY
Complete the Compassion Fatigue Self-Test (Appendix B). List up to 3 items that may be a challenge for you and explain why.

_____

_____

_____

_____

_____

Complete the Self-Care Assessment (Appendix B). How would you rate your current status of self-care? What will you add to your self-care plan?

_____

_____

_____

_____

_____

_____

_____

_____

QUIZ

Name 3 symptoms of compassion fatigue:

    1.   _____

    2.   _____

    3.   _____

Name 3 symptoms of ***organizational*** compassion fatigue:

    1.   _____

    2.   _____

    3.   _____

List 3 ways to prevent compassion fatigue:

    1.   _____

    2.   _____

    3.   _____

RECOVERY PLANNING
Stages of Change/ Recovery Plan Basics

Basics of the recovery plan
Stages of Change and using Motivational Interviewing to begin Recovery Planning

Putting knowledge into practice, this lesson will guide you through using motivational interviewing techniques to create a recovery plan and help clients through stages of change.

✓ To apply the stages of change and motivational interviewing techniques to create the recovery plan.

Reading

+ Review
+ MI Basics handout
+ MI Skills Tip Sheet handout
+ Motivational Strategies handout
+ *Study guide: Using Assessments*
+ SAMHSA TIP 35 (pp 31-34)
+ *Read the entire publication for a more in-depth look at using MI*

What is a recovery plan?
Components of a recovery plan:

✓ _____

✓ _____

✓ _____

✓ _____

✓ _____

✓ _____

Stages of change and using motivational interviewing to begin recovery planning.

ACTIVITY: Invite someone to role play a client and practice identifying the "client's" stage of change and practice using MI skills. Share "client's" feedback of how you did following the activity.

_____

_____

_____

_____

_____

QUIZ

1. A recovery plan serves as a roadmap for a client's recovery.

    a) True.
    b) False.

2. Recovery plans never change once they are written.

    a) True.
    b) False.

For each stage of change, list a motivational interviewing skill that a peer support specialist can employ to help a client to the next stage:

Precontemplation _____

Contemplation _____

Preparation _____

Action _____

Maintenance _____

Relapse _____

Recovery Capital

Recovery capital
Recovery capital assessment

The building blocks of a good recovery plan are made of recovery capital. Clients already have access to this asset, but many of them will have a hard time identifying and developing it.

- ✓ Identify how recovery capital can be developed and rebuilt.
- ✓ Identify models to help develop the recovery plan.

Reading/Assignment

- ✦ *Study guide: Recovery Capital*
- ✦ *Philadelphia: Appendix E: Diversity of Strengths*
- ✦ *Recovery capital: A primer for addiction professionals, White & Cloud 2008*
- ✦ *Recovery capital scale*

Recovery capital

List 3 types of recovery capital and give a concrete example of each:

1. _____
2. _____
3. _____

Recovery capital assessment.

ACTIVITY: Take William White's Recovery Capital Scale. Invite someone to role play a client and practice identifying the "client's" recovery capital. Share "client's" feedback of how you did following the activity.

_____
_____
_____
_____
_____
_____
_____

QUIZ

1. Community recovery capital encompasses community attitudes/policies/resources related to addiction and recovery that promote the resolution of alcohol and other drug problems.

    a)   True.
    b)   False.

2. Personal recovery capital can include how much money I have in the bank.

    a)   True.
    b)   False.

3. Recovery capital includes only a client's external resources.

    a)   True.
    b)   False.

4. To evaluate a client's recovery capital a peer support specialist can do which of the following?

    a)   Talk to the client.
    b)   Give the client the Recovery Capital Scale.
    c)   Investigate the client's life and tell the client what their capital is?
    d)   a and b.

5. Sources of recovery capital might be social support, spirituality and religiousness.

    a)   True.
    b)   False.

Types of Recovery Plans & How to Get There

Lesson Topics

SMART Goals
Wheel of Life
GROW
Strengths-based

Those who plan and write goals have a higher likelihood of success in recovery. There are several types of recovery plans that can be used to guide clients through articulating goals and peer supporters are instrumental in guiding clients through the process of creating a plan as well as sticking to the plan.

- ✓ Demonstrate the ability to write SMART goals.
- ✓ Practice using the Wheel of Life technique.
- ✓ Complete a GROW plan.
- ✓ Identify important elements of the strengths-based approach and how it can be used with clients.

Reading/Assignment

+ *Study guide: Types of Recovery Plans & How to Get There*

SMART Goals:

S _____

M _____

A _____

R _____

T _____

Write 2 SMART goals for yourself:

_____

_____

_____

_____

_____

_____

What is the Wheel of Life used for?

_____

_____

GROW plan

G   _____

R   _____

O   _____

W   _____

How would you help clients identify their strengths?

_____

_____

_____

_____

_____

ACTIVITY: Invite someone to role play a client and guide "client" through each of the above. Share "client's" feedback of how you did following the activity.

_____

_____

_____

_____

_____

QUIZ

1. The "S" in SMART goals standards for "Substance".

    a) True.
    b) False.

2. Effective goals provide a time frame within which they will be achieved.

    a) True.
    b) False.

3. The Wheel of Life can help clients evaluate if there is balance in their life.

    a) True.
    b) False.

Write a SMART goal:

_____

_____

_____

_____

_____

What can a peer support specialist do to help a client identify strengths when they are having difficulty?

_____

_____

_____

_____

_____

Relapse Prevention

Lesson Topics

Relapse Prevention

✓ What is relapse and how do you deal with it in the context of recovery?

Relapse preparation

✓ WRAP®
✓ Relapse Action Plan
✓ Crisis Plan
✓ Advance Directive
✓ Post Crisis Plan

No recovery plan is complete without a relapse prevention component and while relapse cannot always be completely prevented, the negative effects of relapse can be minimized when a plan of action is created to not only identify the warning signs, but also to deal with relapse when it occurs.

✓ To understand relapse and communicate effectively with clients about relapse.
✓ To demonstrate an ability to guide clients through relapse prevention planning.

Reading

✦ *Study guide: Relapse Prevention*
✦ *Why Relapse Isn't a Sign of Failure article*
✦ *The Way WRAP® Works*
✦ *Relapse Action Plan, SAMHSA*

ACTIVITY: Find a partner and practice guiding "client" through a WRAP® plan. Make note of observations and feedback.

_____

_____

_____

_____

_____

QUIZ

Write a paragraph describing how you would explain and normalize relapse for a client.

_____

_____

_____

_____

_____

_____

_____

_____

Part of the WRAP® plan is to identify a client's triggers and develop a plan to deal with them. List 3 potential triggers and an action to deal with it.

_____

_____

_____

_____

_____

1. Which part of the WRAP® plan describes what a client wants to happen in the event a relapse leaves him or her unable to speak for him or herself?

   a)   Daily maintenance plan
   b)   Early warning signs
   c)   Advance Directive
   d)   Post Crisis Plan

SUPPORTING ACTIVITIES
Self-Advocacy

Lesson Topics	Self-advocacy

One of the most powerful lessons a peer supporter can teach a client is that of self-advocacy. Peer supporters empower client with a sense of autonomy and self-efficacy through example and guidance.

- ✓ Describe how self-advocacy is beneficial in recovery and how it can be used with clients.
- ✓ Understand clients' rights during the coaching process.

Reading/Assignment	

+ *Study Guide: Self-Advocacy*
+ *Philadelphia: Section 3, Domains 3 and 4*
+ *Becoming a Self-Advocate article*

Self-advocacy
In what ways have you advocated for yourself?

_____

_____

_____

_____

_____

_____

_____

_____

ACTIVITY: Administer the General Self-Efficacy Scale to a "client" and use it to determine the client's level of self-advocacy. Then list 1-3 ways you would help the client develop self-advocacy skills.

_____

_____

_____

_____

QUIZ

1. Peer support specialists should make clients aware of their rights.

   a) True.
   b) False.

2. Clients have the right to be aware of all treatment options.

   a) True.
   b) False.

3. Allowing a client to help themselves and make their own choices does not allow them to develop a greater sense of self confidence.

   a) True.
   b) False.

4. Advocacy services are typically provided when a client receives services.

   a) True.
   b) False.

Accessing Programs

Lesson Topics

Accessing programs
Advocacy project (optional)

A major task for peer support when guiding clients through empowerment and self-advocacy is connecting them with community resources that can aid in their recovery.

✓ Identify how to access social service programs.

Reading/Assignment

✦ *Study guide: Accessing Programs*

Self-advocacy
In what ways have you advocated for yourself?

_____

_____

_____

_____

_____

_____

_____

_____

_____

ACTIVITY: Administer the General Self-Efficacy Scale to a "client" and use it to determine the client's level of self-advocacy. Then list 1-3 ways you would help the client develop self-advocacy skills.

_____

_____

_____

_____

_____

QUIZ

1. Peer support specialists should make clients aware of their rights.

    a)   True.
    b)   False.

2. Clients have the right to be aware of all treatment options.

    a)   True.
    b)   False.

3. Allowing a client to help themselves and make their own choices does not allow them to develop a greater sense of self confidence.

    a)   True.
    b)   False.

4. Advocacy services are typically provided when a client receives services.

    a)   True.
    b)   False.

Accessing Programs

Accessing programs
Advocacy project (optional)

A major task for peer support when guiding clients through empowerment and self-advocacy is connecting them with community resources that can aid in their recovery.

✓ Identify how to access social service programs.

Reading/Assignment

✦ *Study guide: Accessing Programs*

This session should be highly specialized to the community in which the participant will be working. The goal is to become more aware of community and state resources available to clients, thereby empowering peer support to provide clients with self-advocacy opportunities. Participants are encouraged to complete the suggested advocacy project or to create their own.

For participants who are already in a clinical setting, use this session to discuss how to refer based on their organization's policies.

Cultural Competency & Special Populations (Gerontology)

Lesson Topics	Cultural competency & special populations Gerontology

Recovery is a cultural experience. Learn to become aware of your cultural perceptions and how they impact your work with clients.

- ✓ Increase awareness and understanding of one's cultural perceptions.
- ✓ increase knowledge about the existence of diversity and its influence on recovery.

Reading

Required:
- ✦ *Study guide: Cultural Competency, Gerontology*
- ✦ *Philadelphia: Appendix G: DBHIDS Policy on Services to LGBTQI People*
- ✦ Northeast ATTC Resource Links Volume 7, Issue 2 *Cultural Competency: Its Impact on Addiction Treatment and Recovery*
- ✦ Psychiatric Times article: *Culture and Substance Abuse: Impact of Culture Affects Approach to Treatment*
- ✦ *Gerontology and its impact on mental health*

Cultural competence

Cultural competence is built from two foundations:

- ✔ _____
- ✔ _____

ACTIVITY: With a partner, fill out the ADDRESSING model of culture for each person. Share results with each other and discuss what biases about addiction and recovery one might have based on their self-identified culture. Then write down several observations you have about the experience.

A – age _____

D – disability (born with) _____

D – disability (acquired) _____

R – religion _____

E – ethnicity _____

S – sexual orientation _____

S – socioeconomic status _____

I – indigenous origin (geographic place you come from) _____

N – national origin (the nation/political atmosphere you come from) _____

G – gender _____

Observations/Notes

_____

_____

_____

_____

_____

QUIZ

1. Cultural competence is built from two foundations: Which ones are they?

   a) Awareness and knowledge of one's own culture and cultural biases
   b) Awareness and knowledge of clients and communities
   c) a & b

2. The degree to which an individual identifies with his or her native culture is called

   a) Infiltration
   b) Acculturation
   c) Assimilation
   d) None of the above

Give an example of how culture might affect recovery.

_____

_____

_____

_____

_____

Finding a Job

Finding a job
Guidelines for licensing and certification

Peer support is a growing field full of opportunities. Learn what to look for and create a plan for finding a job.

- ✓ Examine current growth trends in the field.
- ✓ Taking care after training.

Reading

+ *Study Guide: Finding a Job*
+ *Sample job description*

Optional:

+ *Results from a National Survey of Certified Peer Specialist Job Titles and Job Descriptions: Evidence of a Versatile Behavioral Health Workforce*
+ *Peer Specialist Training & Certification Programs: A National Overview*
+ *Peer Recovery Credential Job Analysis Report 2013, IC& RC*

My Job Plan

I will look for jobs that are:

_____

_____

_____

_____

_____

What I want in a job:

_____

_____

_____

_____

_____

What I don't want in a job:

_____

_____

_____

_____

_____

Licensing/certifications I NEED to pursue:

_____

_____

_____

_____

_____

Licensing/certifications I WOULD LIKE to pursue:

_____

_____

_____

_____

_____

Professional self-care plan:

_____

_____

_____

_____

_____

Trauma-Informed Care

Trauma-informed care

The prevalence of trauma in the histories of those in recovery is high and ignoring that history will be detrimental to a client's recovery. Learn about trauma-informed care and how peer supporters can recognize trauma symptoms and refer clients to the help they need.

- ✓ To understand what trauma-informed care is?
- ✓ To be able to recognize a client's need for trauma-informed care and direct clients to appropriate services.

Reading

Required:

+ *Study guide: Trauma Informed Care:*
+ *Philadelphia: Appendix D: Trauma-Informed Care: From Survival to Thriving*
+ Chapter 1 from *Substance Abuse and Mental Health Services Administration. Trauma-Informed Care in Behavioral Health Services. Treatment Improvement Protocol (TIP) Series 57*

How does trauma relate to addiction and recovery?

_____

_____

_____

_____

_____

_____

What are some signs you would look for if a client did not disclose trauma?

_____

_____

_____

_____

_____

QUIZ

1. Most people who have problems with substances also have a history of trauma.

   a) True.
   b) False.

2. Women who are victimized are more likely to have more complex mental health issues which are often compounded by physical health issues.

   a) True.
   b) False.

3. Which of the following are NOT considered aspects of providing trauma informed care?

   a) Creating a safe environment.
   b) Allowing perpetrators of violence to hang around the treatment center.
   c) Promote awareness and understanding of trauma.
   d) Support choice, control and autonomy.

A thin African American adolescent boy walks into your community treatment center. He approaches you at the desk quickly, glancing around him as if he is afraid someone is following him. His shoulders are hunched and when he speaks, he speaks quickly and quietly. As he is asking questions about the program, the phone rings and the young man jumps back as if to protect himself.

What would you do for this client?

_____

_____

_____

Give an example of a strengths based question you could ask him:

_____

_____

_____

The VIA Classification of Character Strengths

1. Wisdom and Knowledge – Cognitive strengths that entail the acquisition and use of knowledge

    ☆ Creativity [originality, ingenuity]: Thinking of novel and productive ways to conceptualize and do things; includes artistic achievement but is not limited to it.

    ☆ Curiosity [interest, novelty-seeking, openness to experience]: Taking an interest in ongoing experience for its own sake; finding subjects and topics fascinating; exploring and discovering.

    ☆ Judgment [critical thinking]: Thinking things through and examining them from all sides; not jumping to conclusions; being able to change one's mind in light of evidence; weighing all evidence fairly.

    ☆ Love of Learning: Mastering new skills, topics, and bodies of knowledge, whether on one's own or formally; obviously related to the strength of curiosity but goes beyond it to describe the tendency to add systematically to what one knows.

    ☆ Perspective [wisdom]: Being able to provide wise counsel to others; having ways of looking at the world that make sense to oneself and to other people.

2. Courage – Emotional strengths that involve the exercise of will to accomplish goals in the face of opposition, external or internal.

    ☆ Bravery [valor]: Not shrinking from threat, challenge, difficulty, or pain; speaking up for what is right even if there is opposition; acting on convictions even if unpopular; includes physical bravery but is not limited to it.

    ☆ Perseverance [persistence, industriousness]: Finishing what one starts; persisting in a course of action in spite of obstacles; "getting it out the door"; taking pleasure in completing tasks

    ☆ Honesty [authenticity, integrity]: Speaking the truth but more broadly presenting oneself in a genuine way and acting in a sincere way; being without pretense; taking responsibility for one's feelings and actions.

    ☆ Zest [vitality, enthusiasm, vigor, energy]: Approaching life with excitement and energy; not doing things halfway or halfheartedly; living life as an adventure; feeling alive and activated.

3. Humanity - Interpersonal strengths that involve tending and befriending others.

    ☆ Love: Valuing close relations with others, in particular those in which sharing and caring are reciprocated; being close to people.

    ☆ Kindness [generosity, nurturance, care, compassion, altruistic love, "niceness"]: Doing favors and good deeds for others; helping them; taking care of them.

☆ Social Intelligence [emotional intelligence, personal intelligence]: Being aware of the motives and feelings of other people and oneself; knowing what to do to fit into different social situations; knowing what makes other people tick.

4. Justice - Civic strengths that underlie healthy community life.

    ☆ Teamwork [citizenship, social responsibility, loyalty]: Working well as a member of a group or team; being loyal to the group; doing one's share.
    ☆ Fairness: Treating all people the same according to notions of fairness and justice; not letting personal feelings bias decisions about others; giving everyone a fair chance.
    ☆ Leadership: Encouraging a group of which one is a member to get things done and at the time maintain time good relations within the group; organizing group activities and seeing that they happen.

5. Temperance – Strengths that protect against excess.

    ☆ Forgiveness: Forgiving those who have done wrong; accepting the shortcomings of others; giving people a second chance; not being vengeful.
    ☆ Humility: Letting one's accomplishments speak for themselves; not regarding oneself as more special than one is?
    ☆ Prudence: Being careful about one's choices; not taking undue risks; not saying or doing things that might later be regretted.
    ☆ Self-Regulation [self-control]: Regulating what one feels and does; being disciplined; controlling one's appetites and emotions.

6. Transcendence - Strengths that forge connections to the larger universe and provide meaning.

    ☆ Appreciation of Beauty and Excellence [awe, wonder, elevation]: Noticing and appreciating beauty, excellence, and/or skilled performance in various domains of life, from nature to art to mathematics to science to everyday experience.
    ☆ Gratitude: Being aware of and thankful for the good things that happen; taking time to express thanks.
    ☆ Hope [optimism, future-mindedness, future orientation]: Expecting the best in the future and working to achieve it; believing that a good future is something that can be brought about.
    ☆ Humor [playfulness]: Liking to laugh and tease; bringing smiles to other people; seeing the light side; making (not necessarily telling) jokes.
    ☆ Spirituality [faith, purpose]: Having coherent beliefs about the higher purpose and meaning of the universe; knowing where one fits within the larger scheme; having beliefs about the meaning of life that shape conduct and provide comfort.

APPENDIX B: Assessments
20 QUESTION SELF- ASSESSMENT FOR HEALTHY BOUNDARIES
Dr. Jane Bolton, PsyD, LMFT - Psychotherapy and Life Coaching

PUT A CHECK IN THE BOX THAT IS MOST ACCURATE	Never	Rarely	Some-times	Often	Almost Always
1. Do you feel stressed out, overwhelmed, burnt out?					
2. Would you do most anything to avoid hurting others?					
3. do you feel as if your kids (mate, parents, others) run your life?					
4. Do you feel as if you are never caught up, or as if your life is not your own.					
5. Do you feel taken advantage of by those you love.					
6. Do you resent others for being so demanding and inconsiderate?					
7. Do others' needs seem much more urgent than yours?					
8. Do you see yourself as the only one who can help, and that you therefore should say yes?					
9. Do you tend to meet others' needs before your own?					
10. Do you question the legitimacy of your own needs?					
11. Do you hate to disappoint others' expectations?					
12. Are you secretly afraid that if you don't do what others ask of you, that they will leave you?					
13. Do you say OK or say nothing when you would rather not to do something for someone, because you don't want a conformation?					
14. Do you deep down believe that if you don't anticipate people's needs and provide services for them, they won't want to be with you?					
15. Do you try to convince yourself that your feeling aren't real, or that you shouldn't have those feelings, or that your feelings don't matter compared to the other person's feelings?					
16. Are you very distressed if one disapproves of you?					
17. Are you very distressed if someone seems as if they don't like you?					
18. if someone criticizes you, do you automatically believe that their criticism is true?					
20. Do you let other people define what your behavior means? (Ex: "you don't really love me if you won't...)					
PUT A CHECK IN THE BOX THAT IS MOST ACCURATE					

Copyright 199. Dr. Jane Bolton, a marriage and family therapist results coach and contemporary psychoanalyst and is dedicated to supporting people in the fullest expression of their Authentic selves. this includes Discovery. Understanding, Acceptance, Expression, and Empowerment of the self. Call 310 838 6363 or visit www.Dr-Jane-Bolton.com

Brief COPE

These items deal with ways you've been coping with the stress in your life since you found out you were going to have to have this operation. There are many ways to try to deal with problems. These items ask what you've been doing to cope with this one. Obviously, different people deal with things in different ways, but I'm interested in how you've tried to deal with it. Each item says something about a particular way of coping. I want to know to what extent you've been doing what the item says. How much or how frequently. Don't answer on the basis of whether it seems to be working or not—just whether or not you're doing it. Use these response choices. Try to rate each item separately in your mind from the others. Make your answers as true FOR YOU as you can.

1 = I haven't been doing this at all
2 = I've been doing this a little bit
3 = I've been doing this a medium amount
4 = I've been doing this a lot

_____ 1. I've been turning to work or other activities to take my mind off things.
_____ 2. I've been concentrating my efforts on doing something about the situation I'm in.
_____ 3. I've been saying to myself "this isn't real.".
_____ 4. I've been using alcohol or other drugs to make myself feel better.
_____ 5. I've been getting emotional support from others.
_____ 6. I've been giving up trying to deal with it.
_____ 7. I've been taking action to try to make the situation better.
_____ 8. I've been refusing to believe that it has happened.
_____ 9. I've been saying things to let my unpleasant feelings escape.
_____ 10. I've been getting help and advice from other people.
_____ 11. I've been using alcohol or other drugs to help me get through it.
_____ 12. I've been trying to see it in a different light, to make it seem more positive.
_____ 13. I've been criticizing myself.
_____ 14. I've been trying to come up with a strategy about what to do.
_____ 15. I've been getting comfort and understanding from someone.
_____ 16. I've been giving up the attempt to cope.
_____ 17. I've been looking for something good in what is happening.
_____ 18. I've been making jokes about it.
_____ 19. I've been doing something to think about it less, such as going to movies, watching TV, reading, daydreaming, sleeping, or shopping.
_____ 20. I've been accepting the reality of the fact that it has happened.
_____ 21. I've been expressing my negative feelings.
_____ 22. I've been trying to find comfort in my religion or spiritual beliefs.
_____ 23. I've been trying to get advice or help from other people about what to do.
_____ 24. I've been learning to live with it.

_____ 21. I've been expressing my negative feelings.
_____ 22. I've been trying to find comfort in my religion or spiritual beliefs.
_____ 23. I've been trying to get advice or help from other people about what to do.
_____ 24. I've been learning to live with it.
_____ 25. I've been thinking hard about what steps to take.
_____ 26. I've been blaming myself for things that happened.
_____ 27. I've been praying or meditating.
_____ 28. I've been making fun of the situation.

Brief COPE Scoring

Scales are computed as follows (with no reversals of coding):

Self-distraction, items 1 and 19
Active coping, items 2 and 7
Denial, items 3 and 8
Substance use, items 4 and 11
Use of emotional support, items 5 and 15
Use of instrumental support, items 10 and 23
Behavioral disengagement, items 6 and 16
Venting, items 9 and 21
Positive reframing, items 12 and 17
Planning, items 14 and 25
Humor, items 18 and 28
Acceptance, items 20 and 24
Religion, items 22 and 27
Self-blame, items 13 and 26

Carver, C. S. (1997). You want to measure coping but your protocol's too long: Consider the Brief COPE. *International Journal of Behavioral Medicine, 4, 92-100.*

General Self-Efficacy Scale

1 = Not at all true   2 = Hardly true   3 = Moderately true   4 = Exactly true

1	2	3	4	I can always manage to solve difficult problems if I try hard enough.
1	2	3	4	If someone opposes me, I can find the means and ways to get what I want.
1	2	3	4	It is easy for me to stick to my aims and accomplish my goals.
1	2	3	4	I am confident that I could deal efficiently with unexpected events.
1	2	3	4	Thanks to my resourcefulness, I know how to handle unforeseen situations.
1	2	3	4	I can solve most problems if I invest the necessary effort.
1	2	3	4	I can remain calm when facing difficulties because I can rely on my coping abilities.
1	2	3	4	When I am confronted with a problem, I can usually find several solutions.
1	2	3	4	If I am in trouble, I can usually think of a solution.
1	2	3	4	I can usually handle whatever comes my way.

Reference:

Schwarzer, R. & Jerusalem, M. (1995). Generalized Self-Efficacy scale. In J. Weinman, S. Wright, & M. Johnston (Eds.), *Measures in health psychology: A user's portfolio. Causal and control beliefs* (pp. 35-37). Windsor, UK: NFER-NELSON.

Modified Mini Screen (MMS)

SECTION A

	YES	NO
1. Have you been consistently depressed or down, most of the day, nearly every day, for the past 2 weeks?	YES	NO
2. In the past 2 weeks, have you been less interested in most things or less able to enjoy the things you used to enjoy most of the time?	YES	NO
3. Have you felt sad, low or depressed most of the time for the last two years?	YES	NO
4. In the past month, did you think that you would be better off dead or wish you were dead?	YES	NO
5. Have you ever had a period of time when you were feeling up, hyper or so full of energy or full of yourself that you got in to trouble or that other people thought you were not your usual self? (Do not consider times when you were intoxicated on drugs or alcohol)	YES	NO
6. Have you ever been so irritable, grouchy or annoyed for several days, that you had arguments, verbal physical fights, or shouted at people outside your family? Have you or others noticed that you have been more irritable or overreacted, compared to other people, even when you thought you were right to act this way?	YES	NO
PLEASE TOTAL THE NUMBER OF "YES" RESPONSES TO QUESTIONS 1-6		

SECTION B

7. Note this question is in 2parts
 	
    a. have you had one or more occasions when you felt intensely anxious, frightened, uncomfortable or uneasy even when most people would not feel that way?   YES   NO
 	
    b. if yes, did these intense feelings get to be their worst withing 10 minute?
    YES   NO
Interviewer: if the answer to BOTH a and b is NO, code the question NO
	YES	**NO**

8. Do you feel anxious or uneasy in places or situation where you might have the panic- like symptoms we just spoke about? Or do you feel anxious or uneasy in situation where help might not be available or escape might be difficult?
 	
Example include:
 	
  ❖ Being in a crowd.
  ❖ Standing in a line.
  ❖ Being alone away from home or alone at home.
  ❖ Crossing a bridge.
  ❖ Traveling in a bus, train or car.
	YES	**NO**

9. Have you worried excessively or been anxious about several things over the past 6 months? Interviewer: If NO to question 9, answer NO to question 10 and proceed to question 11.	**YES**	**NO**
10. Are these worries present most days?	**YES**	**NO**

11. in the past month, were you afraid or embarrassed when other were watching you, or when you were the focus of attention? Were you afraid of being humiliated?
 	
Examples include:
 	
  ❖ Speaking in public.
  ❖ Eating in public or with others.
  ❖ writing while someone watching.
  ❖ Being in social situations.
	YES	**NO**

12. in the past month, have you been bothered by thoughts, impulses, or image that you couldn't get rid of that were unwanted, distasteful, inappropriate, intrusive or distressing?
 	
Examples include:
 	
  ❖ Were you afraid that you would act on some impulse that would be really shocking?
  ❖ Did you worry a lot about being dirty, contaminated or having germs?
	YES	**NO**

SECTION B (CONTINUED)

❖ Did you worry a lot about contaminating others, or that you would harm someone even though you didn't want to? ❖ Did you have any fears or superstitions that you would be responsible for things going wrong? ❖ Were you obsessed with sexual thoughts, images or impulses? ❖ Didi you hoard or collect lots of things? ❖ Did you have religious practice obsessions?	YES	NO
13. in the past month, did you do something repeatedly without being able to resist doing it? Example include: ❖ Washing or cleaning excessively. ❖ Counting or checking things over and over. ❖ repeating, collecting, or arranging things. ❖ other superstitious rituals.	YES	NO
14. Have you ever experienced or witnessed or had to deal with an extremely traumatic event that included death or serious injury to you or someone else? Examples include: ❖ Serious accidents. ❖ Sexual or physical assault. ❖ Terrorist attack. ❖ Being held hostage. ❖ Kidnaping. ❖ Fire. ❖ Discovering a baby. ❖ Sudden death of someone close to you. ❖ war. ❖ Natural disaster.	YES	NO
15. Have you re-experienced the awful event in a distressing way in the past month? Examples Include: ❖ Dreams. ❖ Intense recollections. ❖ Flashbacks. ❖ Physical reactions.	YES	NO
PLEASE TOTAL THE NUMBER OF "YES" RESPONSES TO QUESTIONS 7-15		

SECTION C

16. Have you ever believed that people were spying on you, or that someone plotting against you, or trying to hurt you?	YES	NO
17. Have you ever believed that someone was reading your mind or could hear your thoughts, or that you could actually read someone's mind or hear what another person was thinking?	YES	NO
18. have you ever believed that someone or some force outside of yourself put thoughts in your mind that were not your own, or made you act in a way that was not your usual self? or, have you ever felt that you were possessed?	YES	NO
19. Have you ever believed that you were being sent special messages through the TV, radio, or newspaper? did you believe that someone you did not personally know was particularly interested in you?	YES	NO
20. Have your relatives or friends ever considered any of your beliefs strange or unusual?	YES	NO
21. Have you ever heard things other people couldn't hear, such as voices	YES	NO
22. Have you ever had visions when you were awake or have you ever seen things other people couldn't see?	YES	NO
PLEASE TOTAL THE NUMBER OF "YES" RESPONSES TO QUESTIONS 16-22		

SCORING THE SCREEN

NUMBER OF "YES" RESPONSES FROM SECTION A		
NUMBER OF "YES" RESPONSES FROM SECTION B		
NUMBER OF "YES" RESPONSES FROM SECTION C		
TOTAL NUMBER OF "YES" RESPONSES FROM SECTION A, B AND C • Score $\geq$10, assessment needed • Score $\geq$ 6& $\leq$,9, assessment needed should be determined by treatment team • Score $\leq$, no action necessary unless determined by treatment team		
YES RESPONSE TO QUESTION #4 • If score = 1, assessment is needed		
YES RESPONSE TO QUESTION #14 and #15 • If score = 2, assessment is needed		
SCORE INDICATED NEED FOR AN ASSESSMENT (CIRCLE)	YES	NO
IF NO, DID TREATMENT TEAM DETERMINE THAT AN ASSESSMENT WAS NEEDED (CIRCLE)	YES	NO

SAFE-T

Suicide Assessment Five-step Evaluation and Triage

1
IDENTIFY RISK FACTORS
Note those that can be modified to reduce risk

2
IDENTIFY PROTECTIVE FACTORS
Note those that can be enhanced

3
CONDUCT SUICIDE INQUIRY
Suicidal thoughts, plans, behavior, and intent

4
DETERMINE RISK LEVEL/INTERVENTION
Determine risk. Choose appropriate intervention to address and reduce risk

5
DOCUMENT
Assessment of risk, rationale, intervention, and follow-up

U.S. DEPARTMENT OF HEALTH AND HUMAN SERVICES
Substance Abuse and Mental Health Services Administration
www.samhsa.gov

RISK LEVEL/INTERVENTION

✓ Assessment of risk level is based on clinical judgment, after completing steps 1-3
✓ Reassess as patient or environmental circumstances change

Suicide assessments should be conducted at first contact, with any subsequent suicidal behavior, increased ideation, or pertinent clinical change; for inpatients, prior to increasing privileges and at discharge.

RISK FACTORS
✓ **Suicidal behavior:** history of prior suicide attempts, aborted suicide attempts, or self-injurious behavior
✓ **Current/past psychiatric disorders:** especially mood disorders, psychotic disorders, alcohol/substance abuse, ADHD, TBI, PTSD, Cluster B personality disorders, conduct disorders (antisocial behavior, aggression, impulsivity), Co-morbidity and _recent onset of illness increase risk_
✓ **Key symptoms:** anhedonia, impulsivity, hopelessness, anxiety/panic, global insomnia, command hallucinations
✓ **Precipitants/stressors/Interpersonal:** triggering events leading to humiliation, shame, or despair (e.g, loss of relationship, financial or health status—real or anticipated). Ongoing medical illness (esp. CNS disorders, pain). Intoxication. Family turmoil/chaos. History of physical or sexual abuse. Social isolation
✓ **Change in treatment:** discharge from psychiatric hospital, provider or treatment change
✓ **Access to firearms**
✓ **Family history:** of suicide, attempts, or Axis 1 psychiatric disorders requiring hospitalization

PROTECTIVE FACTORS
Protective factors, even if present, may not counteract significant acute risk
✓ **Internal:** ability to cope with stress, religious beliefs, frustration tolerance
✓ **External:** responsibility to children or beloved pets, positive therapeutic relationships, social supports

SUICIDE INQUIRY
Specific questioning about thoughts, plans, behaviors, intent
✓ **Ideation:** frequency, intensity, duration—in last 48 hours, past month, and worst ever
✓ **Plan:** timing, location, lethality, availability, preparatory acts
✓ **Behaviors:** past attempts, aborted attempts, rehearsals (tying noose, loading gun) vs. non-suicidal self injurious actions
✓ **Intent:** extent to which the patient (1) expects to carry out the plan and (2) believes the plan/act to be lethal vs. self-injurious. Explore ambivalence: reasons to die vs. reasons to live

* For Youths: ask parent/guardian about evidence of suicidal thoughts, plans, or behaviors, and changes in mood, behaviors, or disposition
* Homicide Inquiry: when indicated, esp. in character disordered or paranoid males dealing with loss or humiliation. Inquire in four

---

RISK LEVEL	RISK/PROTECTIVE FACTOR	SUICIDALITY	POSSIBLE INTERVENTIONS
High	Psychiatric diagnoses with severe symptoms or acute precipitating event; protective factors not relevant	Potentially lethal suicide attempt or persistent ideation with strong intent or suicide rehearsal	Admission generally indicated unless a significant change reduces risk. Suicide precautions
Moderate	Multiple risk factors, few protective factors	Suicidal ideation with plan, but no intent or behavior	Admission may be necessary depending on risk factors. Develop crisis plan. Give emergency/crisis numbers
Low	Modifiable risk factors, strong protective factors	Thoughts of death, no plan, intent, or behavior	Outpatient referral, symptom reduction. Give emergency/crisis numbers

(This chart is intended to represent a range of risk levels and interventions, not actual determinations.)

DOCUMENT Risk level and rationale; treatment plan to address/reduce current risk (e.g., medication, setting, psychotherapy, E.C.T., contact with significant others, consultation); firearms instructions, if relevant; follow-up plan. For youths, treatment plan should include roles for parent/guardian.

Name _____ Section _____ Date _____

WELLNESS WORKSHEET II
Major Life Events and Stress

To get a feel for the possible health impact of the various recent events or changes in your life, think back over the past year and circle the points listed for each of the events that you experience during the time.

Health

An injury or illness that:
      kept you in bad a week or more,
      or sent you to the hospital   74
      was less serious than that   44
Major dental work   26
Major change in eating habits   27
Major change in sleeping habits   26
Major change in your usual type or
amount of recreation   28

Work

Change to a new type of work   51
Change in your work hours or conditions   35
change in your responsibilities at work
      more responsibilities   29
      fewer responsibilities   21
      promotion   31
      demotion   42
      transfer   32
Troubles of work
      with your boss   29
      with your co workers   35
      with persons under your supervision   35
      other work trouble   28
Major business adjustment   60
retirement   52
Loss of job
      laid off from work   68
      fired from work   79
online course to help you in your work   18

Home and Family

Major changes in living conditions   42
Change in residence:
      move withing same town or city   25
      move to different town, city, state   47
Change in family get-togethers   25
Major change in health or behavior of
family member   55
Marriage   50
Pregnancy   67
miscarriage or abortion   65
Gain of new family members
      birth of child   66
      adoption of a child   65
      a relative moving in with you   59
spouse beginning or ending work   46
Child leaving home:
      to attend college   41
      due to marriage   41
      for other reason   45
Change in arguments with spouse   50
In-law problems   38
Change in marital status of your parents:
      divorce   59
      remarriage   50
separation from spouse:
      due to work   53
      due to marital problems   76
divorce   96
Birth of grandchild   43
Death of spouse   119
Death of other family member:
      child   123
      brother or sister   102
      parent   100

insel/Roth, Connect Core Concept in Health, Twelfth Edition © 2012 the McGraw-Hill Companies, Inc. Chapter 2
insel/Roth, Connect Core Concept in Health, Brief Twelfth Edition © 2012 the McGraw-Hill Companies, Inc. Chapter 2

WELLNESS WORKSHEET II- continued

Personal and Social

Change in personal habits	26
Beginning or ending school or college	38
Change of school or college	35
Change of political beliefs	24
Change of religious beliefs	29
Change in social activities	27
Vacation trip	24
New, close, personal relationship	37
Engagement to marry	45
Girlfriend or boyfriend problems	39
sexual difficulties	44
Break-up of a close personal relationship	47
An accident	48
Minor violation of the law	20
Being held in jail	75
Death of a close friend	70
Major decision about your immediate future	51
Major personal achievement	36

Financial

Major change in finances:	
increased income	38
decreased income	60
investment or credit difficulties	56
Loss or damage of personal property	43
Moderate purchase	20
Major purchase	37
Foreclosure on a mortgage or loan	58

Total score _____

Scoring: It is important for you to periodically review your self-care, along with your needs and action plans to meet those needs. If you find that you responded with a 1 (Very True) to more than 15 of these items, it's definitely time to take a close and careful look at self-care issues.

SOURCE: Adapted from Miller .M.A., and R.H. Rahe 1997. Life change scaling for the 1990s . *Journal of psychosomatic Research* 43(3); 279-292. copyright 1997, with permission from Elsevier.

Compassion Fatigue Self-Test: An Assessment

Answer the questions below to the best of your knowledge. There is no right or wrong answer. Assign one of these numbers to each one of the questions below:

Responses: 1 = Very True 2 = Somewhat True 3 = Rarely True

You will find summation directions at the end of the test.

1. ___ When people get upset, I try to smooth things out.
2. ___ I am able to listen to other's problems without trying to "fix" them and/or take away their pain.
3. ___ My self-worth is determined by how others perceive me.
4. ___ When I am exposed to conflict, I feel it is my fault.
5. ___ I feel guilty when others are disappointed by my actions.
6. ___ When I make a mistake, I tend to be extremely critical of myself. I have difficulty forgiving myself.
7. ___ I usually know how I want other people to treat me.
8. ___ I tell people how I prefer to be treated.
9. ___ My achievements define my self-worth.
10. ___ I feel anxious in most situations involving confrontation.
11. ___ In relationships, it is easier for me to "give" than to "receive".
12. ___ I can be so focused on someone I am helping that I lose sight of my own perceptions, interests and desires.
13. ___ It is hard for me to express sadness.
14. ___ To make mistakes means that I am weak.
15. ___ It is best to not "rock the boat" or "make waves."
16. ___ It is important to put people at ease.
17. ___ It is best not to need others.
18. ___ If I cannot solve a problem, I feel like a failure.
19. ___ I often feel "used up" at the end of the day.
20. ___ I take work home frequently.
21. ___ I can ask for help but only if the situation is serious.
22. ___ I am willing to sacrifice my needs in order to please others.
23. ___ When faced with uncertainty, I feel that things will get totally out of control.
24. ___ I am uncomfortable when others do not see me as being strong and self-sufficient.
25. ___ In intimate relationships, I am drawn to people who are needy or need me.
26. ___ I have difficulty expressing my differing opinion in the face of an opposing viewpoint.
27. ___ When I say "no," I feel guilty.
28. ___ When others distance from me, I feel anxious.
29. ___ When listening to someone's problems, I am more aware of their feelings than I am of my own feelings.

30. ____ I find it difficult to stand up for myself and express my feelings when someone treats me in an insensitive manner.
31. ____ I feel anxious when I am not busy.
32. ____ I believe that expressing resentments is wrong.
33. ____ I am more comfortable giving than receiving.
34. ____ I become anxious when I think I've disappointed someone.
35. ____ Work dominates much of my life.
36. ____ I seem to be working harder and accomplishing less.
37. ____ I feel most worthwhile and alive in crisis situations.
38. ____ I have difficulty saying "no" and setting limits.
39. ____ My interests and values reflect what others expect of me rather than my own interests and values.
40. ____ People rely on me for support.

Scoring:
It is important for you to periodically review your self-care, along with your needs and action plans to meet those needs. If you find that you responded with a 1 (Very True) to more than 15 of these items, it's definitely time to take a close and careful look at self-care issues.

Used with permission. Copyright 1996: Dennis Portnoy, from OVEREXTENDED AND UNDERNOURISHED: A SELFCARE GUIDE FOR PEOPLE IN HELPING ROLES. All rights reserved. For more information, go to www.myselfcare.org.

Self-Care: An Assessment

Consider the following 40 statements below, filling in the blanks that follow with the number that best corresponds with your life at this time.

Responses: 1 = Very True 2 = Somewhat True 3 = Rarely True

1. When people get upset, I try to smooth things out. _____

2. I am able to listen to others problems without trying to "fix" them and/or take away their pain. _____

3. My self-worth is determined by how others perceive me. _____

4. When I am exposed to conflict, I feel it is my fault. _____

5. I feel guilty when others are disappointed by my actions. _____

6. When I make a mistake, I tend to be extremely critical of myself: I have difficulty forgiving myself. _____

7. I usually know how I want other people to treat me. _____

8. I tell people how I prefer to be treated. _____

9. My achievements define my self-worth. _____

10. I feel anxious in most situations involving confrontation. _____

11. In relationships, it is easier for me to "give" that to "receive". _____

12. I can be so focused on someone I am helping

    that I lose sight of my own perceptions, interests and desires. _____

13. It is hard for me to express sadness. _____

14. To make mistakes means that I am weak. _____

15. It is best to not "rock the boat" or "make waves". _____

16. It is important to put people at ease. _____

17. It is best not to need others. _____

18. If I cannot solve a problem, I feel like a failure. _____

19. I often feel "used up" at the end of the day. _____

20. I take work home frequently. _____

21. I can ask for help but only if the situation is serious. _____

22. I am willing to sacrifice my needs in order to please others. _____

23. When faced with uncertainty, I feel that things will get totally out of control. _____

24. I am uncomfortable when others do not see me as being strong and self-sufficient. _____

25. In intimate relationships, I am drawn to people who are needy or need me. _____

26. I have difficulty expressing my differing opinion in the face of an opposing viewpoint. _____

27. When I say "no", I feel guilty. _____

28. When others distance from me, I feel anxious. _____

29. When listening to someone's problems, I am more aware of their feelings than I am of my own feelings. _____

30. I find it difficult to stand up for myself and express my feelings when someone treats me in an insensitive manner. _____

31. I feel anxious when I am not busy. _____

32. I believe that expressing resentments is wrong. _____

33. I am more comfortable giving than receiving. _____

34. I become anxious when I think I've disappointed someone. _____

35. Work dominates much of my life. _____

36. I seem to be working harder and accomplishing less. _____

37. I feel most worthwhile and alive in crisis situations. _____

38. I have difficulty saying "no" and setting limits. _____

39. My interests and values reflect what others expect of me rather than my own interests and values. _____

40. People rely on me for support. _____

It is important for you to periodically review your self-care, along with your needs and action plans to meet those needs. If you find that your responded with a 1 (Very True) to more than 15 of these items, it's definitely time to take a close and careful look at self-care issues.

Used with permission. Copyright 1996: Dennis Portnoy, from OVEREXTENDED AND UNDERNOURISHED: A SELFCARE GUIDE FOR PEOPLE IN HELPING ROLES. All rights reserved. For more information, go to www.myselfcare.org.

Recovery Capital Scale

Place a number by each statement that best summarizes your situation.

> 5. Strongly Agree
> 4. Agree
> 3. Sometimes
> 2. Disagree
> 1. Strongly Disagree

____ I have the financial resources to provide for myself and my family.

____ I have personal transportation or access to public transportation.

____ I live in a home and neighborhood that is safe and secure.

____ I live in an environment free from alcohol and other drugs.

____ I have an intimate partner supportive of my recovery process.

____ I have family members who are supportive of my recovery process.

____ I have friends who are supportive of my recovery process.

____ I have people close to me (intimate partner, family members, or friends) who are also in recovery.

____ I have a stable job that I enjoy and that provides for my basic necessities.

____ I have an education or work environment that is conducive to my long-term recovery.

____ I continue to participate in a continuing care program of an addiction treatment program, (e.g., groups, alumni association meetings, etc.)

____ I have a professional assistance program that is monitoring and supporting my recovery process.

____ I have a primary care physician who attends to my health problems.

____ I am now in reasonably good health.

____ I have an active plan to manage any lingering or potential health problems.

____ I am on prescribed medication that minimizes my cravings for alcohol and other drugs.

____ I have insurance that will allow me to receive help for major health problems.

____ I have access to regular, nutritious meals.

____ I have clothes that are comfortable, clean and conducive to my recovery activities.

____ I have access to recovery support groups in my local community.

____ I have established close affiliation with a local recovery support group.

____ I have a sponsor (or equivalent) who serves as a special mentor related to my recovery.

____ I have access to online recovery support groups.

____ I have completed or am complying with all legal requirements related to my past.

____ There are other people who rely on me to support their own recoveries.

____ My immediate physical environment contains literature, tokens, posters or other symbols of my commitment to recovery.

____ I have recovery rituals that are now part of my daily life.

____ I had a profound experience that marked the beginning or deepening of my commitment to recovery.

____ I now have goals and great hopes for my future.

____ I have problem solving skills and resources that I lacked during my years of active addiction.

____ I feel like I have meaningful, positive participation in my family and community.

____ Today I have a clear sense of who I am.

____ I know that my life has a purpose.

____ Service to others is now an important part of my life.

____ My personal values and sense of right and wrong have become clearer and stronger in recent years.

Possible Score: 175
My Score: _____

The areas in which I scored lowest were the following:

1. _____
2. _____
3. _____
4. _____
5. _____

Recovery Capital Plan

After completing and reviewing the Recovery Capital Scale, complete the following. In the next year, I will increase my recovery capital by doing the following:

Goal # 1: _____
Goal # 2: _____
Goal # 3: _____
Goal # 4: _____

My Recovery Capital "To Do" List

In the next week, I will do the following activities to move closer to achieving the above goals:

1. _____
2. _____
3. _____
4. _____
5. _____

Course Evaluation

Appendix C - Personal reflection project

Write a personal narrative to include strengths and weaknesses. Explain how your experiences will benefit you as a peer recovery support specialist or recovery coach.

_____

_____

_____

_____

_____

_____

_____

_____

_____

_____

_____

_____

_____

_____

_____

_____

_____

_____

_____

_____

_____

_____

_____

_____

Explain your philosophy of recovery and how your approach will benefit clients.

_____

_____

_____

_____

_____

_____

_____

_____

_____

_____

_____

_____

_____

_____

_____

_____

_____

_____

_____

_____

_____

_____

_____

Following assessments, create a recovery plan with your "client." The recovery plan could include:

- ✓ 2 SMART goals
- ✓ Wheel of Life
- ✓ GROW Plan
- ✓ List of client strengths
- ✓ List of recovery capital
- ✓ WRAP® Plan
- ✓ 3 action steps

Explain which recovery plan items you used and why:

_____

_____

_____

_____

_____

_____

_____

_____

_____

_____

_____

_____

_____

_____

_____

_____

_____

_____

_____

_____

Appendix D- Sample client project

Take another person through a first meeting and choose 2 assessments to give them. Write a report documenting your first meeting, including a brief client history, client's goals for recovery and assessment results.

_____

_____

_____

_____

_____

_____

_____

_____

_____

_____

_____

_____

_____

_____

_____

_____

_____

_____

_____

_____

_____

_____

Request feedback from your partner and write down 3 things you did well and 3 things you can improve upon.

_____

_____

_____

_____

_____

_____

_____

_____

_____

_____

Create SMART goals based upon feedback.

_____

_____

_____

_____

_____

_____

_____

_____

_____

_____

Appendix E - Advocacy project (optional)

Identify and connect with another treatment provider. Find out if they are taking new clients, their policies for clients, their expectations of clients in treatment and their willingness to work with a recovery coach.

Describe what you learned:

_____

_____

_____

_____

_____

_____

_____

_____

Research social services in your area, including HIV/AIDS testing, welfare, food stamps, child care, transportation, disability, unemployment, healthcare and wellness programs in your county and state. Find a suicide prevention hotline in your region. Develop an understanding of how to access these agencies, including contact information and eligibility requirements.

Describe what you learned:

_____

_____

_____

_____

_____

_____

_____

_____

_____

_____

References

Abrahams, I. A., Ali, O., Davidson, L., Evans, A. C., King, J. K., Poplawski, P., & White, W.L. (2014). *Practice guidelines for recovery and resilience oriented treatment.* Philadelphia: City of Philadelphia Department of Behavioral Health and Mental Retardation Services.

Bolton, J. (1999). 20 *Question Self-Assessment for Healthy Boundaries.* Culver City, CA: Psychotherapy to Live Life Fully. Retrieved from http://www.dr-jane-bolton.com/support-files/boundary-assessment.pdf

Carver, C. S. (1997). You want to measure coping but your protocol's too long: Consider the Brief COPE. *International Journal of Behavioral Medicine,* 4, 92-100.

Center for Substance Abuse Treatment (1999). *Enhancing Motivation for Change in Substance Abuse Treatment.* Treatment Improvement Protocol (TIP) Series, No. 35. HHS Publication No. (SMA) 13-4212. Rockville, MD: Substance Abuse and Mental Health Services Administration.

Center for Substance Abuse Treatment (2008). *Medication-assisted therapies: Providing a whole-patient approach to treatment* (Radio Show). National Recovery Month. Retrieved from http://www.recoverymonth.gov/Resources-Catalog/2008/Radio-Cast/Medication-Assisted-Therapies.aspx

Center for Substance Abuse Treatment (2009). *What are Peer Recovery Support Services? HHS Publication No. (SMA) 09-4454.* Rockville, MD: Substance Abuse and Mental Health Services Administration.

Compassion Fatigue Awareness Project (2013). *Recognizing Compassion Fatigue.* Retrieved from http://www.compassionfatigue.org/pages/symptoms.html.

Copeland Center for Wellness & Recovery (2014). T*he Way WRAP® Works.* Brattleboro, VT: Copeland Center.

Copeland, M.E. (2012). The Wellness Recovery Action Plan (WRAP®). *Copeland Center for Wellness and Recovery.* Retrieved July 17, 2013 from http://copelandcenter.com/what- wrap/history-wrap.

Deegan, P. (2012). *Personal medicine worksheet whole health version.* Retrieved from https://www.recoverylibrary.com/browse/recovery#personal-medicine-worksheets

Freedman, M. N. & McCaughan, A. M. (2008). HIPAA for dummies: A practitioner's guide. In G.R. Walz, J.C. Blueuer, & R. K. Yep (Eds). *Compelling counseling interventions: Celebrating VISTAS' fifth anniversary* (pp. 305-312), Ann Arbor, MI: Counseling Outfitters.

Gagne, C., Oliver, J. & Davis, L. (2009) *Equipping behavioral health systems & authorities to promote peer specialist/peer recovery coaching services,* Rockville, MD: Center for Mental Health Services and the Center for Substance Abuse Treatment, Substance Abuse and Mental Health Services Administration, US Department of Health and Human Services.

Grohol, J. (2009). 15 Common Cognitive Distortions. *Psych Central.* Retrieved July 31, 2013, from http://psychcentral.com/lib/15-common-cognitive-distortions/0002153

Grohol, J. (2009). Fixing Cognitive Distortions. *Psych Central.* Retrieved July 31, 2013, from http://psychcentral.com/lib/fixing-cognitive-distortions/0002154

Hays, P. A. (2001). Addressing cultural complexities in practice: A framework for clinicians and counselors. Washington, D. C. : American Psychological Association. Retrieved from http://cultureandhealth.wordpress.com/2009/12/29/addressing-understanding-the-social-construct-of-power/

Hazelden Foundation (2013). *Modified Mini-Screen*. Retrieved from
http://www.bhevolution.org/public/screening_tools.page?menuheader=4

Hoge M.A., Morris J.A., Laraia M., Pomerantz A., & Farley, T. (2014). *Core Competencies for Integrated Behavioral Health and Primary Care*. Washington, DC: SAMHSA - HRSA Center for Integrated Health Solutions.

Insel, P. & Roth W. T., (2012). Wellness Worksheets. In *Connect Core Concepts in Health Twelfth Edition Chapter 2*. The McGraw-Hill Companies, Inc.

International Association of Peer Supporters (2013). *National Ethical Guidelines and Practice Standards: National Practice Guidelines for Peer Supporters. Sparta,* MI.

International Coach Federation. (2013). Core Competencies. *ICF: International Coach Federation*. Retrieved from http://www.coachfederation.org/credential/landing.cfm?ItemNumber=2206&navItemNumber=576

International Coach Federation. (2013). Ethics & Regulation. *ICF: International Coach Federation*. Retrieved from http://www.coachfederation.org/about/ethics.aspx?ItemNumber=850&navItemNumber=621

International Credentialing & Reciprocity Consortium (2013). *IC&RC Leading the world in credentialing*. Retrieved from www.internationalcredentialing.org/about

Kaufman, L., Brooks, W., Steinley-Bumgarner, M., & Stevens-Manser, S. (2012). *Peer Specialist Training and Certification Programs*: A National Overview. Austin, TX: University of Texas at Austin Center for Social Work Research.

Kelley-Hardison, J. & Goldberg, S. (2014). *Lived Experience*. Atlanta, GA: PARfessionals.

Kunkel, T. (2012). *Substance abuse and confidentiality*: 42 CFR Part 2. Williamsburg, VA: National Center for State Courts.

McKregg, K. & Oakden, J. (2009). *Characteristics of good peer support*. Wellington, New Zealand: Wellink Trust. Retrieved from http://www.wellink.org.nz/pdf/Characteristics_of_Good_Peer_Support.pdf

Mid-Atlantic Addiction Technology Transfer Center, Motivational Interviewing Website. *An overview of motivational interviewing*. Retrieved from http://motivationalinterview.org/Documents/1%20A%20MI%20Definition%20Principles%20&%20Approach%20V4%20012911.pdf

Mid-Atlantic Addiction Technology Transfer Center, Motivational Interviewing Website. Skills tip sheet. Retrieved from http://www.motivationalinterview.org/Documents/Skills%20Tip%20Sheet.pdf

Mid-Atlantic Addiction Technology Transfer Center, Motivational Interviewing Website. *MI Basics*. Retrieved from www.motivationalinterview.org.

Mindtools, Ltd. (2013). The Wheel of Life: Finding balance in your life. *Mindtools*. Retrieved from http://www.mindtools.com/pages/article/newHTE_93.htm#

National Alliance on Mental Illness (2013). Becoming a self-advocate. Strength of Us. Retrieved July 13, 2013 from http://strengthofus.org/pages/view/156/.

National Institute on Drug Abuse (2010). *Drugs, Brains, and Behavior: The Science of Addiction (NIH Publication No. 10-5605)*. National Institutes of Health, U.S. Department of Health and Human Services. Retrieved from http://www.drugabuse.gov/sites/default/files/sciofaddiction.pdf

Northeast ATTC Resource Links Volume 7, Issue 2 *Cultural competency: Its impact on addiction treatment and recovery.*

Peterson, C., & Seligman, M. E. P. (2004). *Character strengths and virtues: A handbook and classification. New York:* Oxford University Press and Washington, DC: American Psychological Association. www.viacharacter.org

Pfizer, A. (2014). *Gerontology and its impact on mental health.* Atlanta, GA: PARfessionals.

Portnoy, D. (1996). Compassion fatigue self-test: An assessment from *Overextended and undernourished: A selfcare guide for people in helping roles.* MN: Hazelden. Retrieved from www.myselfcare.org

Portnoy, D. (1996). Self-care: An assessment from *Overextended and undernourished: A selfcare guide for people in helping roles.* MN: Hazelden. Retrieved from www.myselfcare.org

Purdue University (n.d.). Everything you ever wanted to know about case notes. *Student Resources.* Retrieved from http://www.purdue.edu/hhs/hdfs/engagement/documents/MFT_forms/Student/Resources/Casenote.PDF

Quesenbery, W. & Brooks, K. (2010). *10 Skills for Active Listening from Storytelling* for User Experience. New York: Rosenfeld Media. Retrieved from http://www.rosenfeldmedia.com/books/storytelling/

Recovery Coaches International (2013). Core competencies. *Recovery Coaches International: The voice of choice for recovery and beyond.* Retrieved from http://www.recoverycoaching.org/content.aspx?page_id=22&club_id=263697&module_id=142736

Sack, D. (2012). *Why relapse isn't a sign of failure.* Retrieved from http://www.psychologytoday.com/blog/where-science-meets-the-steps/201210/why-relapse-isnt-sign-failure

Sample job description. Adapted from Peer Support Technician VACO Classified (Veteran's Administration)

Samurovich, G. (2014). *Legal overview for peer supporters.* Atlanta, GA: PARfessionals.

Schwarzer, R. & Jerusalem, M. (1995). Generalized Self-Efficacy scale. In J. Weinman, S. Wright, & M. Johnston (Eds.), M*easures in health psychology: A user's portfolio. Causal and control beliefs* (pp. 35-37). Windsor, UK: NFER-NELSON.

Schwenk, E.B., Brusilovskiy, E., & Salzer, M.S. (*2009). Results from a national survey of certified peer specialist job titles and job descriptions: Evidence of a versatile behavioral health workforce.* The University of Pennsylvania Collaborative on Community Integration: Philadelphia, PA.

Substance Abuse and Mental Health Services Administration (2002). *Action Planning for Prevention & Recovery.* HHS Publication No. (SMA) 3720. Rockville, MD: Substance Abuse and Mental Health Services Administration.

Substance Abuse and Mental Health Services Administration (2009). *SAFE-T Suicide Assessment Five-step Evaluation and Triage* (HHS Publication No. (SMA) 09-4432). Washington, DC: U.S. Government Printing Office. Retrieved from http://store.samhsa.gov/shin/content/SMA09-4432/SMA09-4432.pdf

Substance Abuse and Mental Health Services Administration (2012). *Whole Health Action Management (WHAM) Peer Support Training Participant Guide.* Washington, DC: USGovernment Printing Office. Retrieved from http://www.integration.samhsa.gov/health-wellness/wham

Substance Abuse and Mental Health Services Administration (2014). *Trauma-Informed Care in Behavioral Health Services*. Treatment Improvement Protocol (TIP) Series 57. HHS Publication No. (SMA) 13-4801. Rockville, MD: Substance Abuse and Mental Health Services Administration.

University of Kentucky (2014). So what is *"self care"*? Retrieved from https://www.uky.edu/StudentAffairs/VIPCenter/downloads/self%20care%20defined.pdf

VIA Institute on Character (2004). *VIA Classification of Character Strengths*. Retrieved from http://www.viacharacter.org/www/Character-Strengths/VIA-Classification

Wang, Z. G. (2013). *Peer Recovery Credential Job Analysis Report 2013*. Harrisburg, PA: International Certification & Reciprocity Consortium.

Westermeyer J. (2004). Cross-cultural aspects of substance abuse. In: Galanter, M., & Kleber, H.D., eds. *Textbook of Substance Abuse Treatment*. Arlington, VA: American Psychiatric Publishing.

White, W. L. (1999). A lost world of addiction treatment. *Counselor,* 17(2), 8-11.

White, W., the PRO-ACT Ethics Workgroup, with legal discussion by Popovits R. & Donohue, B. *(2007). Ethical Guidelines for the Delivery of Peer-based Recovery Support Services. Philadelphia: Philadelphia Department of Behavioral Health and Mental Retardation Services.*

White, W. & Cloud, W. (2008). Recovery capital: A primer for addictions professionals. *Counselor, 9(5),* 22-27.

White, W. L. (2008). *Recovery management and recovery-oriented systems of care: Scientific rationale and promising practices.* Northeast Addiction Technology Transfer Center, the Great Lakes Addiction Technology Transfer Center, and the Philadelphia Department of Behavioral Health.

White, W. (2011). *A chronology of moderation societies and related controversies.* Posted at www.williamwhitepapers.com

White, *W. Recovery capital scale.* Retrieved from http://www.williamwhitepapers.com/pr/Recovery%20Capital%20Scale.pdf

Made in United States
Orlando, FL
13 January 2023